ARACHNID WORLD

WOLF SPIDERS

SANDRA MARKLE

MOTHERS ON GUARD

L LERNER PUBLICATIONS COMPANY MINNEAPOLIS

FOR CURIOUS KIDS EVERYWHERE

ACKNOWLEDGMENTS

The author would like to thank Dr. Matthew Persons, Susquehanna University, Selinsgrove, Pennsylvania; Dr. George Uetz, University of Cincinnati, Cincinnati, Ohio; and Dr. Simon Pollard, Canterbury Museum, Christchurch, New Zealand, for sharing their expertise and enthusiasm. A special thanks to Skip Jeffery for his support during the creation of this book.

Lerner Publications Company
A division of Lerner Publishing Group, Inc.
241 First Avenue North
Minneapolis, MN 55401 U.S.A.

Website address: www.lernerbooks.com

Library of Congress Cataloging-in-Publication Data

Markle, Sandra.
    Wolf spiders : mothers on guard / by Sandra Markle.
      p.   cm. — (Arachnid world)
    Includes bibliographical references and index.
    ISBN 978–0–7613–5040–8 (lib. bdg. : alk. paper)
     1. Wolf spiders—Juvenile literature. I. Title.
  QL458.42.L9M327 2011
  595.4′4—dc22   2010004273

Manufactured in the United States of America
1 – DP – 12/31/10

CONTENTS

WELCOME TO THE WORLD OF ARACHNIDS

(ah-RACK-nidz). Arachnids can be found in every habitat on Earth except in the deep ocean.

So how can you tell if an animal is an arachnid rather than a relative like a horseshoe crab shown below? Both belong to a group of animals called arthropods (AR-throh-podz). The animals in this group share some traits. They have bodies divided into segments, jointed legs, and a stiff exoskeleton. This is a skeleton on the outside like a suit of armor. But one way to tell if an animal is an arachnid is to count its legs and body parts. While not every adult arachnid has eight legs, most do. Arachnids also usually have two main body parts. Adult horseshoe crabs have ten legs and a shell divided into three body parts.

This book is about wolf spiders. Like all spiders, they're hunters. They also produce a liquid poison called venom. Unlike most spiders though, wolf spiders work very hard at being parents. Female wolf spiders, like the Carolina wolf spider *(right)*, are super moms.

WOLF SPIDER FACT

A wolf spider's body temperature rises and falls with the temperature around it. So it must warm up to be active.

YOUNG SPIDERS

There are more than two thousand different kinds of wolf spiders. They all share certain features. They all have two main body parts: the cephalothorax (sef-uh-loh-THOR-ax) and the abdomen. A waistlike part called the pedicel joins the two. The spider's exoskeleton is made up of many plates connected by stretchy membranes. This lets it bend and move.

Take a close look at the outside of this female wolf spider, called *Trochosa* (troh-KOH-za), to discover other key features wolf spiders share.

SPINNERETS:
These parts spin the spider's silk.

LEGS:
These are used for walking.

ABDOMEN

PEDICEL

EYES:
These sensory organs detect light and send messages to the brain for sight. Wolf spiders have eight eyes. Two of the eyes are much larger than the others.

CHELICERAE (KEH-liss-er-eye):
These are a pair of strong, jawlike parts near the mouth. They have a sawlike edge to crush and tear and end in fangs to inject venom.

PEDIPALPS:
These are a pair of leglike parts that extend from the head near the mouth. They help catch prey and hold it for eating. In males the pedipalps are also used during reproduction.

CEPHALOTHORAX

ON THE INSIDE

Look inside an adult female wolf spider.

VENOM GLAND: This body part produces venom.

HEART: This muscular tube pumps blood toward the head. The blood flows throughout the body spaces and returns to the heart.

BRAIN: The brain receives messages from body parts and sends signals back to them.

SUCKING STOMACH: The stomach works with the pharynx to move food between the mouth and the gut.

PHARYNX (FAR-inks): This muscular tube pumps food into the stomach. Hairs in it help filter out any solid bits.

NERVE GANGLIA: These bundles of nerve tissue carry messages between the brain and other body parts.

COXAL (KAHK-sel) GLANDS: These are special groups of cells that collect liquid wastes and pass them through openings to the outside of the body.

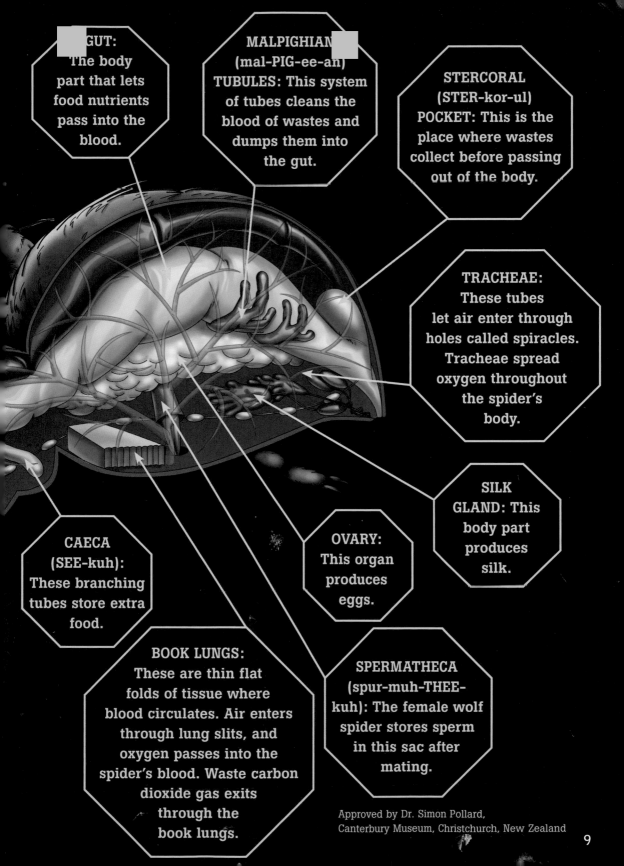

GUT: The body part that lets food nutrients pass into the blood.

MALPIGHIAN (mal-PIG-ee-an) TUBULES: This system of tubes cleans the blood of wastes and dumps them into the gut.

STERCORAL (STER-kor-ul) POCKET: This is the place where wastes collect before passing out of the body.

TRACHEAE: These tubes let air enter through holes called spiracles. Tracheae spread oxygen throughout the spider's body.

SILK GLAND: This body part produces silk.

CAECA (SEE-kuh): These branching tubes store extra food.

OVARY: This organ produces eggs.

BOOK LUNGS: These are thin flat folds of tissue where blood circulates. Air enters through lung slits, and oxygen passes into the spider's blood. Waste carbon dioxide gas exits through the book lungs.

SPERMATHECA (spur-muh-THEE-kuh): The female wolf spider stores sperm in this sac after mating.

Approved by Dr. Simon Pollard, Canterbury Museum, Christchurch, New Zealand

BECOMING ADULTS

Like all arachnids, wolf spiders go through incomplete metamorphosis. *Metamorphosis* means "change." A wolf spider's life includes three stages: egg, nymph or spiderling, and adult. Compare the Carolina wolf spiderlings to the adult female.

SOME KINDS OF ARTHROPODS, SUCH AS INSECTS, GO THROUGH COMPLETE METAPHORPHOSIS. The four stages are egg, larva, pupa, and adult. Each stage looks and behaves very differently.

WOLF SPIDER FACT

The adult Carolina wolf spider's body length is 1.3 inches (3.5 centimeters). The spiderling is much smaller.

SPIDERLINGS

ADULT FEMALE

As a little spiderling eats, it grows bigger. When its exoskeleton becomes tight, it needs to molt. Then this armorlike covering splits open, and the spiderling crawls out. Its new exoskeleton is soft at first. The spiderling forces blood into different parts of its body to stretch the soft exoskeleton. After the exoskeleton hardens, the spiderling will have room to grow before it needs to molt again. Besides getting bigger, a spiderling can sometimes regenerate, or grow a new part, such as a leg that was injured and broke off.

If the body part is lost through an injury at the beginning of a growth period, a new part develops, folded up, inside the injury site. The part unfolds the next time the spiderling molts. The regenerated part may be a little shorter or thinner. But it will work just like the original.

WOLF SPIDER FACT

A spider's exoskeleton is made of a material similar to human fingernails. The new exoskeleton is folded up, to some extent, under the old one.

MOLTED EXOSKELETON

HUNTING PARENTS

BUILT TO HUNT

The focus of a wolf spider's life is hunting and producing babies. Wolf spiders mainly hunt by ambushing (hiding and then attacking) their prey. They wander until they spot prey. Or they travel until they find clues, such as a smaller spider's silk or an insect's wastes. These clues show that prey is in the area. Then the spider stays still and waits. A wolf spider's vision helps it hunt. Wolf spiders, like this burrowing wolf spider *(right)*, have eight eyes. Two large eyes look forward. Below them, four smaller eyes nearly span the width of the wolf spider's head. Two more eyes are on top of its head. So a wolf spider can look up, down, to the right and left, and straight ahead all at once.

WOLF SPIDER FACT

Wolf spiders can't move their eyes the way people do. When they look at something, they have to turn their whole body to focus on it.

A wolf spider's coloring also helps it ambush prey. The spider's body is colored to blend in where it naturally lives, such as in a sandy desert or a forest. Just by staying still, a wolf spider, like a brush-legged wolf spider, can hide in plain sight.

A wolf spider's body, like this Carolina wolf spider, is covered with sensory hairs. Some of these help a wolf spider taste what it touches. Others alert it to air movements. There are also lots of tiny slits in a wolf spider's exoskeleton. Each slit has a special sensor. They let the spider feel the slightest movement in whatever surface it's touching. Together these two kinds of sensors help the wolf spider track prey. They also help it sense a bigger predator that could be hunting it.

Once it sees prey, a wolf spider moves fast. This insect is just over an inch (3 cm) away when the Brazilian wolf spider attacks. ZING! The spider's fangs pierce the insect's exoskeleton. The wolf spider injects venom from a tiny hole near each fang tip. This kills the prey so fast it doesn't have a chance to struggle or to injure its attacker. Then the spider starts to eat. Wolf spiders first hunt to get the energy they need to grow up. Then they hunt to get energy to find a mate and produce young.

WOLF SPIDER FACT

Like all spiders, wolf spiders have such small mouths only liquid food can pass through to their stomachs. Hairs in the pharynx help filter out any solid bits.

THE FATHER'S JOB

Male wolf spiders, like this thin-legged wolf spider *(right)*, have one job to do. They have to find a mate. It isn't easy. For a small spider, walking over the ground can be like crawling through a huge jungle. Before a male sets out to find a mate, he spins a tiny web. He crawls over this and deposits his sperm (male reproductive cells) on it. He picks up the sperm with his pedipalps. Then he goes in search of a mate, carrying his sperm packet.

When a wolf spider travels, it pulls a silk line, called a dragline, from its spinnerets. From time to time, it touches its rear end to the ground and makes a gluey silk to anchor the line. This dragline is also a good way to send messages. Adult female wolf spiders who are ready to mate coat their draglines with pheromones. Pheromones are chemical signals. They help males find females. A thin-legged male wolf spider searches until it finds a thin-legged female's dragline. Then the male follows this trail. When he finds the female, he moves closer slowly. He taps the ground and waves his legs to signal he's courting. Once she lets him come close, he inserts his sperm into her gonopore.

WOLF SPIDER FACT

Male wolf spiders coat their draglines with a different kind of chemical signal. These chemicals repel other males.

THE MOTHER'S JOB

Female wolf spiders have to produce lots of eggs. The females are bigger than males. They need to be bigger in order to catch bigger prey. They need extra food to give them the energy they need to produce so many eggs.

After she has mated, this female funnel web wolf spider keeps hunting for about a week. She needs the added food energy for her eggs to develop. Then she spins a silk disk. She deposits her eggs one at a time on this disk. As each egg cell leaves her body through her gonopore, it passes the male's sperm stored in the spermatheca. When egg and sperm merge, a baby spider starts to develop. A tough coating forms around the egg cell. Once all the eggs are laid, the female wolf spider spins again. She wraps her eggs in a silk sac. Silk is tough and water resistant, so it protects her eggs. Completing her egg sac doesn't mean the female wolf spider's job is done, however.

FUNNEL WEB WOLF SPIDER

ALL HER EGGS IN ONE SAC

Female wolf spiders carry their egg sac with them while the babies develop inside. This female Brazilian wolf spider spins sticky silk she uses to glue the egg sac to her spinnerets.

Imagine carrying something that weighs one-third your body weight! That's how heavy the egg sac is for the female wolf spider. It's also a big package to carry. The female wolf spider carries her egg sac with her while she hunts, eats, and rests. She also stays alert for predators, like hunting wasps. If she is attacked by a wasp, she defends her egg sac from it.

WOLF SPIDER FACT

Tiny wolf spiders, such as the pirate wolf spider, lay as few as eight to ten eggs in each egg sac. Large wolf spiders, such as the Carolina wolf spider, lay over one thousand.

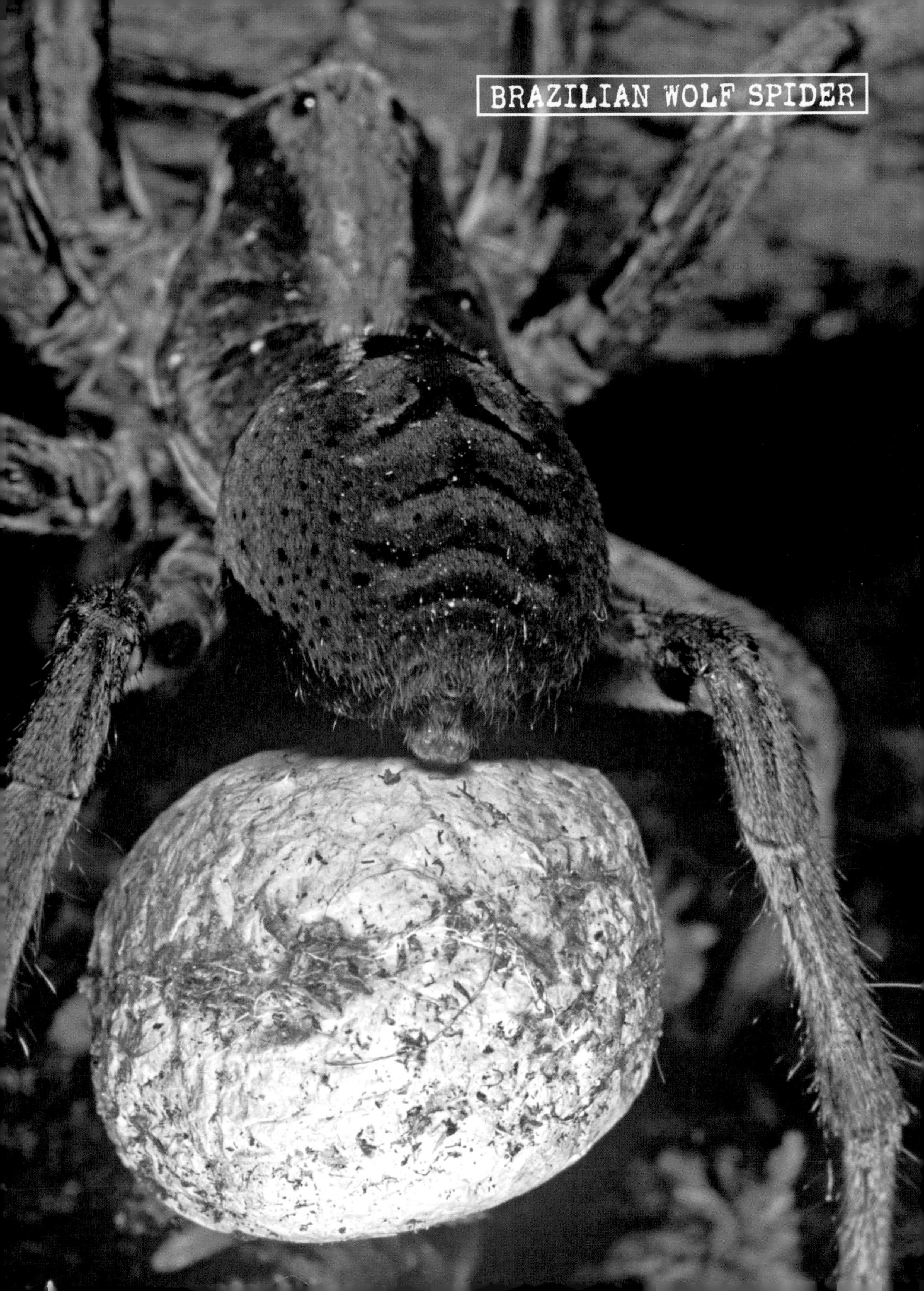
BRAZILIAN WOLF SPIDER

SPIDERLINGS ON BOARD

Inside their egg sac, these spotted wolf spider babies develop for about three weeks. They receive the energy they need from their egg's yolk, which is stored food. Just before they hatch, the babies eat the leftover yolk. Even after the spiderlings hatch, they stay inside their egg sac. They live off their egg yolk while they develop a little more. After the wolf spiderlings molt for the first time, they're ready to leave the egg sac. They chew the silk walls of the sac to make an opening in it. Their mother may also bite it to help break it open. Then the wolf spiderlings crawl out.

The youngsters immediately climb onto their mother's abdomen. The female wolf spider's job isn't over yet.

WOLF SPIDER FACT

The spiderlings cling to special hooked hairs on their mother's abdomen to keep from falling off.

Packed on her back, the spotted wolf spiderlings ride along
with their mother. If any drop off, they hurry to climb on board
again. The spiderlings stay with her for another week or two.
She doesn't give them any food or share the prey she catches.
The spiderlings still have enough stored yolk to keep on
growing. They'll grow big enough to molt a second time before
they have to keep themselves safe. Their mother is only about
0.3 inches (0.8 cm) long. But she's much bigger than they are.
She also knows how to stay alert for predators. Just being with
her helps the spiderlings get a better start than they would
have on their own.

When the spiderlings finally climb down to leave, they quickly run away *(below)*. Once they leave her, the female no longer defends them. She'll eat any she can catch. The biggest, strongest spiderlings also sometimes get a first meal by eating a brother or a sister.

HUNTING TO GROW UP

This spotted wolf spiderling escapes its family and starts to hunt. Suddenly it senses movements that signal something even tinier is nearby. It keeps still and waits. When the insect is close enough for the spiderling to see it, the young spider runs fast and pounces. It bites, injecting venom to make the kill. Then the spiderling uses its strong jaws with the jagged edges to crush and mash its prey. It also throws up digestive juices to break down the insect's soft body parts. The spiderling then sucks in its prey as a liquid meal. It eats until only broken bits of the insect's exoskeleton remain.

WOLF SPIDER FACT

Wolf spiders have caeca, branching parts of their gut, that store food. So they can go long periods without catching prey and eating.

It's late summer, and there are lots of small insects to catch and eat. The spotted wolf spiderling grows bigger. It molts, shedding its old covering. A new exoskeleton is ready underneath. This is soft at first. Because the soft spiderling could be hurt by struggling prey, it sits still and doesn't hunt until its exoskeleton hardens. Once the exoskeleton has hardened, it is large enough for the spiderling to grow bigger before it has to molt again. It will molt at least five times before it becomes an adult, ready to mate.

WOLF SPIDER FACT

Wolf spiders no longer grow bigger or molt once they become adults.

Not all wolf spiders survive to become parents. Some are caught and eaten by predators, like this toad. Some become prey for other spiders. Still others die because it becomes too hot or too cold or they drown in heavy rains.

Spiderlings that live where winters are harsh may not have time to completely grow up in the summer. They find a sheltered spot under a bit of bark or inside a rock crack. There they rest when it's too cold to be active. They come out to hunt only on days when the weather warms up. Not much prey is out during the winter, so some of the spiderlings run out of energy and die before spring. Only a few spiderlings from each egg sac survive to become adults.

WOLF SPIDER FACT

It's important for the spider to find shelter that lets its body stay moist. Drying out can kill the spider.

THE CYCLE CONTINUES

This adult male spotted wolf spider is one of those survivors. He's searching for a mate. Finally, he crosses the dragline of a female spotted wolf spider. He follows her track. When he gets close, he holds up his pedipalps and waves them. It's a signal to her. Wolf spider males are smaller than females. He needs to make sure she sees he's a mate, not a meal.

As long as the female stays still, the male continues to move toward her. When he reaches her, he uses his pedipalps to insert his sperm into her gonopore.

FEMALE   MALE

Once he's mated, the male wolf spider's parenting job is done. However, the female's parenting job is just beginning. It's an around-the-clock job that she does alone. First, the wolf spider mother carries the egg sac. When her babies hatch, she lets them climb on her back and ride along to keep them safe for a while. Those that survive to become adults will one day become hardworking parents. Generation after generation, the wolf spider's cycle of life continues.

SPOTTED WOLF SPIDER

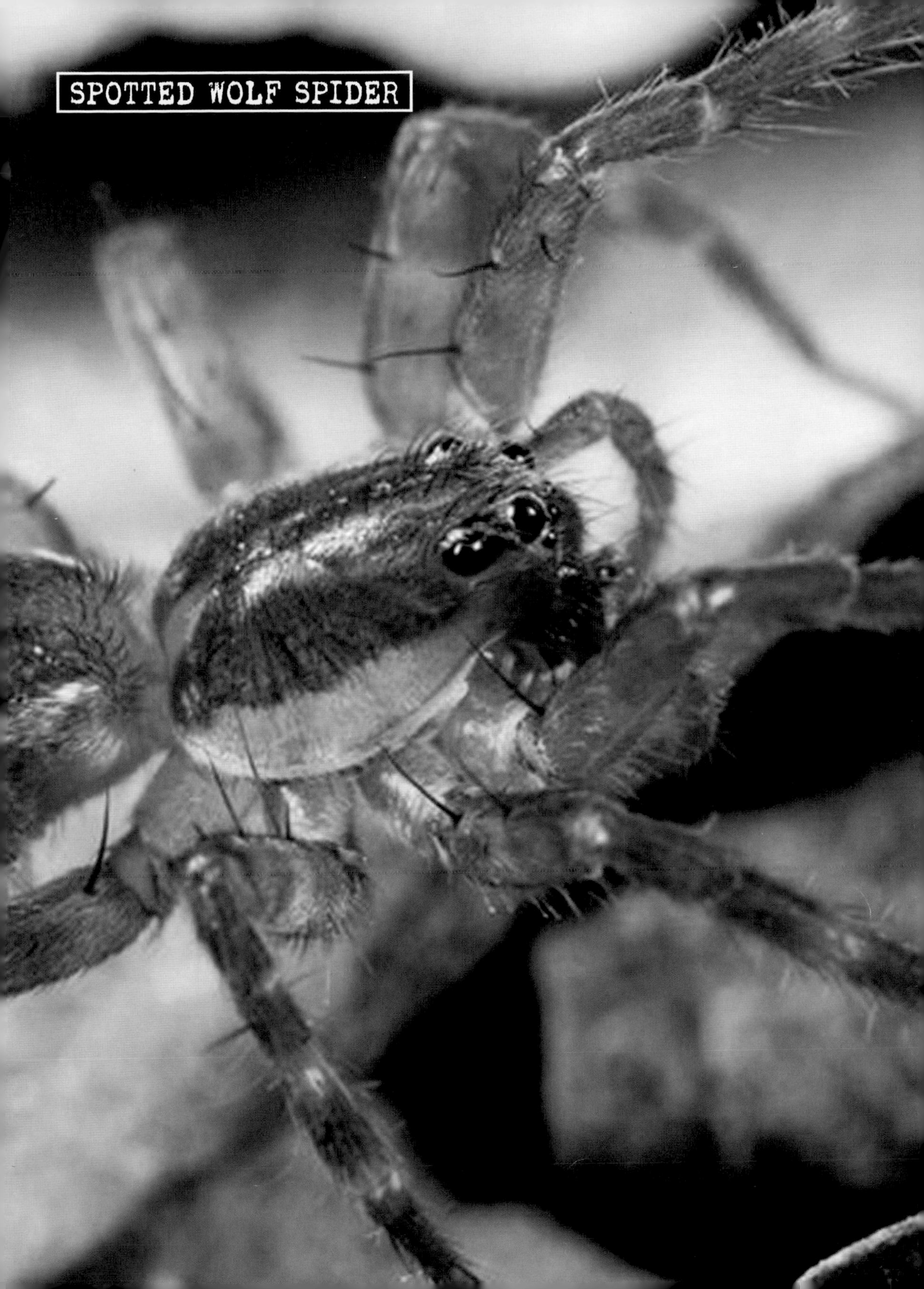

WOLF SPIDERS AND OTHER ARACHNID PARENTS

WOLF SPIDERS BELONG TO A GROUP, or order, of arachnids called Aranea (ah-RAN-ee-ay). These are the spiders. Wolf spiders belong to a family of spiders, the Lycosidae (lie-KOH-seh-die). There are over two thousand different kinds worldwide.

SCIENTISTS GROUP living and extinct animals with others that are similar. So wolf spiders are classified this way:

> kingdom: Animalia
> phylum: Arthropoda
> class: Arachnida
> order: Araneae
> family: Lycosidae

HELPFUL OR HARMFUL? Wolf spiders are mainly helpful. They eat lots of insects. They help control the numbers of insects that could otherwise become pests. Wolf spiders only bite people in self-defense. Like all spiders, though, their bite injects venom. Wolf spider venom usually causes swelling and mild pain. Some people may have an allergic reaction to any spider's bite.

HOW BIG IS a spotted wolf spider? A female's body is about 0.31 inches (8 millimeters) long. Males are about 0.23 inches (6 mm) long.

MORE ARACHNID PARENTS

Compare the care provided by wolf spider mothers to these other arachnid parents.

Emperor scorpion females, like all scorpions, provide protection for

their eggs. They do this by holding them inside their bodies until the young, called scorplings, hatch. Then, one at a time, the young are released through the gonopore. The scorplings climb up the mother's legs and stay on her back until they molt. After that they leave to hunt for themselves. Emperor scorpion females sometimes provide a little extra care for their young. When these scorpion mothers catch and crush insects (such as crickets), they let their scorplings share this meal.

Harvestmen females often guard their eggs. In a few species of

harvestmen (such as *Goniosoma longipes*), the males protect the eggs from predators. These males may guard eggs in a nest they build. Or they may defend an area where females have deposited eggs. The males of one species (*Leytpodoctis oviger*) carry the eggs, stuck onto their fourth leg, until the spiderlings hatch.

Whip scorpion (also called a vinegaroon) females dig a burrow and lay

as many as thirty-five eggs. The female stays with her eggs, guarding them from predators until they hatch. The mother doesn't provide food for her young, but she keeps them safe by letting them stay with her inside the burrow. After they molt, the nymphs go off on their own.

GLOSSARY

abdomen: the rear end of an arachnid. It contains systems for digestion, reproduction, and silk production.

adult: the reproductive stage of an arachnid's life cycle

book lungs: thin, flat folds of tissue where blood circulates. Air enters through slits and passes between these tissue folds, allowing oxygen to enter the blood. Waste carbon dioxide gas exits through them.

brain: the organ that receives messages from body parts and sends signals to them

caeca: branching tubes through which liquid food passes and where extra food is stored

cephalothorax: the front end of an arachnid. It includes the mouth, the brain, and the eyes, if there are any. Legs are also attached to this part.

chelicerae: a pair of strong, jawlike parts that extend from the head in front of the mouth and end in fangs to inject venom. In wolf spiders, the chelicerae have a sawlike edge to crush and tear.

coxal glands: special groups of cells for collecting and getting rid of liquid wastes through openings to the outside of the body. They aid in maintaining water balance in the body.

egg: a female reproductive cell; also the name given to the first stage of an arachnid's life cycle

exoskeleton: the protective, armorlike covering on the outside of an arachnid's body

eyes: sensory organs that detect light and send signals to the brain for sight

fangs: a pair of toothlike parts of the spider's chelicerae. Venom flows out of the fangs through holes near the tip.

gut: a body part through which food nutrients pass into the blood and are carried throughout the body

heart: the muscular tube that pumps blood throughout the body

Malpighian tubules: a system of tubes that cleans the blood of wastes and dumps them into the intestine

molt: the process of an arachnid shedding its exoskeleton

nerve ganglia: bundles of nerve tissue that send messages between the brain and other body parts

ovary: the body part that produces eggs

pedicel: the waistlike part in spiders that connects the cephalothorax to the abdomen

pedipalps: a pair of leglike body parts that extends from the head near the mouth. These help catch prey and hold it for eating. In males the pedipalps are also used during reproduction.

pharynx: a muscular body part that contracts to create a pumping force, drawing food into the body's digestive system. Hairs filter out any solid waste bits.

pheromones: chemical scents given off as a form of communication

regeneration: to regrow a lost body part

silk gland: the body part that produces silk

sperm: a male reproductive cell

spermatheca: the sac in female arachnids that stores sperm after mating

spiderling: the name given to the stage between egg and adult in spiders

spinneret: the body part that spins silk

spiracle: a small opening in the exoskeleton that leads into the trachea

stercoral pocket: a place where wastes collect before passing out of the body

sucking stomach: a muscular body part that, along with the pharynx, pulls liquid food into the arachnid's gut. Cells in the lining produce digestive juices.

tracheae: tubes that help spread oxygen throughout the spider's body. They also store oxygen.

venom: liquid poison

venom gland: the body part that produces venom

DIGGING DEEPER

To keep on investigating wolf spider, explore these books and online sites.

BOOKS

Bishop, Nic. *Nic Bishop Spiders*. New York: Scholastic, 2007. Nic Bishop's amazing photographs provide a great way to explore how wolf spiders are similar to other spiders—and how they're different.

Cooper, Jason. *Wolf Spiders*. Vero Beach, FL: Rourke Publishing, 2006. Take another look at wolf spiders.

Markle, Sandra. *Sneaky Spinning Baby Spiders*. New York: Walker, 2008. Compare how wolf spiderlings hatch and grow up to the life cycles of other kinds of spiders.

Simon, Seymour. *Spiders*. New York: Smithsonian/HarperCollins, 2007. This is a scientific survey of the spider world with gorgeous photos.

Singer, Marilyn. *Venom*. Minneapolis: Millbrook Press, 2007. Find out about creatures that can harm or even kill with a bite or sting.

Souza, D. M., *Packed with Poison!* Minneapolis: Millbrook Press, 2006. Learn about the most venomous and poisonous animals in the world.

Squires, Ann U. *Spiders*. New York: Scholastic, 2003. Look at the various spider babies described in this book and compare them to wolf spiders.

MORE FROM SANDRA MARKLE

INSECT WORLD:
Diving Beetles
Hornets
Locusts
Luna Moths
Mosquitoes
Praying Mantises
Stick Insects
Termites

WEBSITES

Kentucky Spiders

http://www.uky.edu/Ag/CritterFiles/casefile/spiders/wolf/
wolf.htm#hogna

Explore this site to compare wolf spiders to other kinds of spiders.
Don't miss the interactive "Spider Anatomy" page.

Wolf Spider Mama

http://www.youtube.com/watch?v=93VJ4838SoY

Watch an amazing video of a female wolf spider laying eggs. See her
build her egg sac, and watch newly hatched baby spiders in action.
This is a segment of David Attenborough's *Life in the Undergrowth*.

Wolf Spiders: Lycosidae

http://www.biokids.umich.edu/critters/Lycosidae/

Check out facts and photos about wolf spiders.

LERNER SOURCE™

Visit www.lernersource.com
**for free, downloadable arachnid
diagrams, research assignments
to use with this series, and
additional information about
arachnid scientific names.**

WOLF SPIDER ACTIVITY

Female wolf spiders, like this spotted wolf spider, carry their egg sacs with them. They carry them wherever they go and whatever they do—even hunting prey. Follow these steps to get a feel for how hard a wolf spider mom works to protect her developing young.

1. Work with an adult partner to blow up balloons. Stuff a backpack full of them. Pretend this is your egg sac.

2. Slip on the backpack. Carry it with you wherever you go. Keep it on while you eat, play, watch TV, and even sleep, if you can.

3. Try to get through an entire day without any of the balloons popping. If you're up to the challenge, see how many days in a row you can be active and keep the eggs safe in your sac. A female wolf spider carries her egg sac for about three weeks.

BONUS CHALLENGE: Cut out ten circles of colored paper. Make each about 3 inches (7 cm) across. Have your adult partner use loops of masking tape to stick these onto your back. These are your pretend spiderlings. Again, go about your normal activities, but keep the roll of masking tape with you. Anytime one of your spiderlings drops off, stick it on again. Try to keep all ten babies safely on your back for at least three hours. While you're doing this, remember some kinds of wolf spiders have hundreds of babies.

INDEX

PHOTO ACKNOWLEDGMENTS

The images in this book are used with the permission of: © Marilyn & Maris Kazmers/SeaPics.com, p. 4; © Joe Warfel/Eighth-Eye Photography, pp. 5, 13, 17, 36, 38–39; © Bryan E. Reynolds, pp. 6–7, 21; © Dr. Gary Gaugler/Visuals Unlimited, Inc., p. 7; © Independent Picture Service, pp. 8–9; © Nature's Images/Photo Researchers, Inc., pp. 10–11; © Gary Meszaros/Photo Researchers, Inc., pp. 14–15; © João Paulo Burini, pp. 16, 18–19, 29; © Larry West/Bruce Coleman, Inc./Photoshot, pp. 22-23 © Francesco Tomasinelli/Natural Visions, p. 25; © Ken Preston-Mafham/Premaphotos, pp. 26–27, 46–47; © Kim Taylor/naturepl.com, p. 28; © N. A. Callow/NHPA/Photoshot, pp. 30–31; © Gerry Cambridge/NHPA/Photoshot, pp. 32–33; © Gary Meszaros/Visuals Unlimited, Inc., p. 35; © Steve Hopkin/ardea.com, p. 37; © Karl H. Switak/Photo Researchers, Inc., p. 41 (top); © Stephen Dalton/Minden Pictures, p. 41 (middle); © James Carmichael, Jr./NHPA/Photoshot, p. 41 (bottom).

Front cover: © Daniel Heuclin/NHPA/Photoshot.